JCW

Cumberland Island has been described as one of "Georgia's Gems." Its precious nature as a barrier island protects the mainland from erosion, provides habitats for animal and plant life, and renews one's spirit by displaying a rare and genuine beauty.

Published by:
World Publications

For book orders, please contact:

World Publications
Postal Box 24339
Tampa, FL 33623

© 1986 World Publications
Third Edition
L.C. No. 85-51860
ISBN: 0-911977-03-1
Manufactured in Singapore

Acknowledgements
A special thanks to the staff of Cumberland Island National Seashore especially Kenneth O. Morgan, Janis H. Davis, Don Hooker, and Cliff Kevill and to anyone who has worked to preserve the island's character for future generations.

CUMBERLAND ISLAND
A Treasure of Memories

Photography, Text, and Design by
Larry F. Andrews, H. Grant Rice, and Joanne C. Werwie

After several years of backpacking cameras and tripods to Cumberland Island, the authors viewed their photographs as a treasure to be shared. Their book is a collection of these photos depicting some of the island's history, its ecosystems, and unique pristine beauty. It was designed as a keepsake for those who have visited Cumberland Island or for those who just enjoy nature at its best. The cover shot was the first island photo taken as the trio crossed Grand Avenue on their way to Sea Camp. With backpacks in place, cameras mounted atop tripods, they were ready for the unexpected scene. The sensitivity the photographers display in their everyday professions (Larry — physical therapist, Grant — prosthetist, and Joanne — pediatric nurse) is also evident in their desire to ... Gems including ... d.

This book is dedicated to my father with whom I have traveled many of life's trails.

Larry F. Andrews

This book is dedicated in loving memory ... my father whose dream to one day write a book was never realized. His sense of adventure and respect for life has inspired me to share my love of nature.

Joanne C. Werwie

... children, Todd, Kevin, and Jill, who joined me at times on visits to Cumberland Island. Hopefully later in their lives, they will recall some of the memories we shared together.

H. Grant Rice

Carolina wren building nest in jacket

Sea Camp Campsite

Backpackers must carry all their food and essential gear to their designated campsite to prepare for the unpredictable adventures produced by Mother Nature. Wildlife may surprise visitors anywhere on the island including the campsite.

Southern toad

Female cardinal

Top: Prothonotary warbler
Middle: Saw palmetto
Bottom: Pileated woodpecker

Sea Camp forest scene

Maritime forests of live oak and saw palmetto provide a home and refuge for a variety of animal life.

Gray squirrel

Nine-banded armadillo

A raccoon takes a break from his usual mischievous lifestyle. Nestled high among the branches of a live oak tree and a cushion of resurrection fern, he succumbs to an afternoon siesta.

Nesting Carolina Wren

JCW

If observed and not disturbed, most animals and birds will continue their normal activities.

Southern chorus frog

Five-lined skink

Yellow rat snake

No repeat performances can
be requested when viewing a
Cumberland Island sunrise.
Each one creates its own
lingering memory.

Top: American oystercatcher
Middle: Ruddy turnstone
Bottom: Sanderling

When strolling on the beach, note the variety of birds and their almost constant search for food.

Sanderlings and sandpipers feeding on beach

Gulls display their agility on the wing as they easily catch food particles while airborne.

Walking the beach at night can be eerie, especially when the ghost crab hauntingly appears on the sand. If threatened, he will quickly retreat to his burrow.

Nature's designs can be discovered on the dunes and beaches of Cumberland Island. The displays are always changing with the ebb and flow of the tides. Many patterns appear as the lines, shapes, and hues created by an artist with his paintbrush.

Above: Sea oats
Left: Starfish

Clam shell and whelk

Clam Shells

Starfish

Pen Shell

Various life cycles can also be witnessed by the keen observer. North end beaches provide a secluded nesting area for loggerhead turtles.

During the English occupation of Cumberland Island around 1736, a hunting lodge named Dungeness was constructed on the southern end of the island. In the late 1700's, the first mansion at Dungeness was built. The existing ruins are those of the second mansion which was built in the late 1800's by Thomas Carnegie, brother of the financier, Andrew Carnegie.

Chicken and pheasant houses

Some of the automobiles
used in earlier days now rest
in peace under the oak trees.

HGR

Grazing horse with egret

Wild turkeys roaming grounds of Dungeness

Myrtle warblers at water hole.

Dungeness is home for many animals. Wild horses share the area with many small birds and the elusive island turkeys. The male turkey is an attractive bird. His bluish head, red wattle, tassle-like beard, and iridescent, bronze body feathers are more prominently displayed than on the female turkey.

Though easily found at Dungeness, turkeys prefer to be observed from a distance. Anyone trying to get a closer look may be disappointed when the turkeys swiftly trot away to safer surroundings.

Male turkey

Female turkey

23

Grazing horses at Dungeness

Through the cemetery gates at Dungeness, the south marsh and its activities can be viewed.

Female ruby-crowned kinglet

Red-winged blackbird

The photographer alarms an immature, yellow-crowned night heron making its way toward the dock's far end before flying to the protective marsh grasses.

Immature yellow-crowned night heron

Salt marsh

Salt marsh with fiddler crabs

Fiddler crab

Raccoon in marsh

To many creatures, the saltwater marsh means food. While many animals are hidden, horses, raccoons, fiddler crabs, ibis and herons can be seen busily searching for a nourishing meal.

Great egret at rookery

Rookeries for many wading birds may be miles from their daytime feeding sites in the saltwater marsh.

LFA

Above: Ibis in flight
Left: Ibis feeding in salt marsh

The acute senses of the vulture allow no life forms to go unnoticed.

Brown pelican dead on beach

The nesting sites of herons and ibis, and the rejuvenation of resurrection ferns after a rain are evidence of nature's balance between island life and death.

Above Left: Great egret on nest with young
Above Right: Immature ibis & black-crowned heron at rookery
Left: Yellow-crowned night herons near nesting site
Far Left: Resurrection fern

A boardwalk links the dense canopy of live oaks at Sea Camp with the beach as it crosses over and between the fragile sand dunes. Coastal weather and grazing animals can alter a dune's size and shape.

JCW

HGR

LFA

33

Cumberland Island has many natural zones progressing from beaches to foredunes, meadows, inner dunes, live oak forests and marshes.

Marsh grasses washed ashore by ocean tides line the beach and trap blowing sands to create foredunes. This allows sea oats and other vegetation to take root. Sea oats help to form and stabilize the dunes by holding sand with their intricate root systems. Without dunes, the existence of the island would be threatened by erosion.

Photographed in 1980

With the passage of time, massive
dunes at the island's south end
move westward encroaching upon
the marsh.

Dune migration can also be seen from the protective boardwalk. Sand dunes almost completely engulf the cottage as seen in the photo above. Several years later, scenic dunes flank the rear of the same cottage.

Blowing sands and salty sea mist combine to create the gnarled distortions of many trees. The merging of the dunes with the live oaks shows the constant struggle between the forces of sea and land.

HGR

As fatigue sets in, a weary backpacker envisions himself befriending a grazing horse or perhaps a burro to assist him in reaching his final destination.

Grand Avenue, the island's main connector, runs almost the entire 16-mile length of Cumberland Island.

DUCK HOUSE TRAIL

JCW

Duck House Trail crosses over the Sweetwater Lake Complex and sawgrass marsh – an ideal habitat for all forms of wildlife. A road once traveled by hunters now provides the patient and quiet hiker an opportunity to see herons, ibis, ducks, and deer.

An abandoned hunting lodge called Duck House is being reclaimed by the forces of nature. The wooden structure is slowly decaying. Massive dunes are invading the territory, and wildlife roams the old residence.

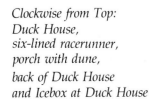

Clockwise from Top:
Duck House,
six-lined racerunner,
porch with dune,
back of Duck House
and Icebox at Duck House

ICW

LFA

Left: Violet wood sorrel
Above: Cloudless sulphur on thistle

Wildflowers make their debut in all seasons, but the greatest display is during spring and summer. The flowers are rich in nectar and attract many butterflies.

Left: Gulf fritillary and cloudless sulphur on thistle
Below: Gulf fritillary on thistle

Top: Cloudless sulphur butterfly
Left: Salvia
Above: Lupine

Opposite Page,
Left: Virginia spiderwort
Top Right: Japanese umbrella mushroom
Bottom Right: Salt marsh pink

SOUTH CUT TRAIL

As the hiker leaves the beach and crosses the dunes at South Cut Trail, he passes wetlands covered with duckweed and water lilies. A wide variety of vegetation and wildlife is present in these areas.

Above: Dune at South Cut Trail
Middle Top: Water lily
Middle Bottom: Alligator & solitary sandpiper
Below: American alligator

Above top: Moss-covered snapping turtle
Bottom: Freshwater pond

49

JCW

Roller Coaster Trail displays an encore of beauty to anyone who detours from South Cut Trail. Cumberland Island seasons set the stage for ever–changing ecosystems.

Top Right: White Ibis silhouette
Right: Maleberry

JCW

LFA

Freshwater pond

Fresh water, in the form of ponds and artesion wells, attracts an assortment of birds and animals.

Left: Green anole
Top Left: Yellow-throated warbler
Top Right: Northern parula warbler
Middle Above: Southern leopard frog
Right: Swallowtail butterfly

Lake Whitney is the largest body of fresh water on Cumberland Island. Great blue herons and osprey are commonly seen feeding at the lake. A lucky hiker may catch a glimpse of the rarely seen glossy ibis.

HGR

Opposite Page:Glossy ibis near Lake Whitney
Opposite Inset: White ibis & glossy ibis at Lake Whitney

Above: Osprey
Right: Great blue heron
Below: Lake Whitney

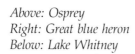

Below and Right: Baptist church at Halfmoon Bluff

1ST A.B. CHURCH
Founded 1893 by
Rev. T. Lockett.
Deacons
W. M. Alberty
C. Trimings
P. Mitchel.
Officers 1937
C. Alberty
P. Trimings
N. Merrou
Beulah G. Alberty
Chu. Clk.
Rev. L. Morrison.
Pastor.
Carved by Geo. H. Leapheart

This Baptist Church at Halfmoon Bluff is still a place of worship today for some island residents.

Huge oak trees shade Grand Avenue and the historical structures of Greyfield Inn and Plum Orchard.

Plum Orchard

Oak trees on Grand Avenue

Greyfield Inn

Below: Resurrection fern
Bottom: Shoelace fern

This large oak tree at the northern end of the island would be of interest to the botanist because it hosts a variety of ferns, moss, and fungi. Here, the photographer focuses on the rare shoelace fern.

From Terrapin Point, one can see the remnants of the Cumberland Wharf — a debarkation point for island visitors from 1870 to 1920.

Part of Cumberland's northern end is hilly with a steep, sandy bluff contrasting the flat marshlands at the southern tip and western side of the island.

This pine forest near Stafford Beach is evidence of man's visible presence. The precise pine-tree planting replaces the once abundant hardwoods harvested by earlier inhabitants of the island. Following years of growth, these trees appear to create an image of a Gothic cathedral.

After an early morning rain,
the sun brightens the darkened
forest to create a mood for
spiritual reflection.

*Forest scene at
Sea Camp*

The evening sky silhouettes the once busy docks at Dungeness and Sea Camp. Near the island visitor center, a view of Cumberland Sound through moss-covered oaks and saw palmetto provides a welcome feeling of rest and tranquility.

Miller's dock at St. Mary's Waterfront (The departure point to Cumberland Island.)